A Poppy Is
to Remember

Heather Patterson ● Ron Lightburn

North Winds Press
A Division of Scholastic Canada Ltd.

The illustrations in this book were painted with oil on Arches paper.

The text was set in 20 point Esprit Book.

The publisher wishes to thank The Royal Canadian Legion, Dominion Command Headquarters, for use of the poppy shown on page 28.

Photo credits: P. 26 (lower): Lt.-Col. John McCrae, National Archives of Canada, C-022873; P. 27 (upper): Mike Drew, *Calgary Sun*; P. 27 (lower): Photograph by Joseph Mokler, reproduced with the permission of Veterans Affairs Canada, 2004; P. 28: Unveiling of Canada's National Memorial at Vimy Ridge – Pilgrims gather in front of the Monument after the Ceremony, Vimy Ridge, France, July 26, 1936, National Archives of Canada, PA-183544; P. 29 (upper): "Wait for me, Daddy": Private Jack Bernard, B.C. Regiment (Duke of Connaught's Own Rifles) saying goodbye to his five-year-old son Warren, New Westminster, B.C., 1940. Photographer: Claude P. Dettloff, National Archives of Canada, C-038723, courtesy of Mrs. D. Joan Macpherson; P. 29 (lower): Courtesy of the family of Private Arthur A. Clarke, 2nd Battalion, Essex Scottish Regiment; P. 30 (upper): Courtesy of Dean and Gail Munroe; P. 30 (lower): Linda Gordon, courtesy of The Royal Canadian Legion, Branch 54, Sooke, B.C.

National Library of Canada Cataloguing in Publication

Patterson, Heather, 1945-
A poppy is to remember / Heather Patterson ; Ron Lightburn, illustrator.

ISBN 0-439-96786-4

1. Remembrance Day (Canada)—Juvenile literature. 2. Poppies—Juvenile literature.
3. Canada—History, Military—Juvenile literature.
4. Canada—Armed Forces—Juvenile literature. I. Lightburn, Ron II. Title.

D680.C2P38 2004   j394.264   C2004-900879-X

6 5 4 3   Printed and bound in Canada   05 06 07 08

For Serena, and a peaceful world

— H.P.

For David, and for all those who keep
the peace around the world

— R.L.

Once there was a long and terrible war
— a war some called the Great War.
Many young men went off to fight,
and many did not return home
to their families.

3

But still, in the muddy fields where they fought, wild poppies sprang up, glowing brightly.

An army doctor, weary from tending
the wounded, wrote a poem about that war,
and about those poppies.

In Flanders Fields

In Flanders fields the poppies blow
Between the crosses, row on row,
That mark our place; and in the sky
The larks, still bravely singing, fly
Scarce heard amid the guns below.

We are the Dead. Short days ago
We lived, felt dawn, saw sunset glow,
Loved, and were loved, and now we lie
In Flanders fields.

Take up our quarrel with the foe:
To you from failing hands we throw
The torch, be yours to hold it high.
If ye break faith with us who die
We shall not sleep, though poppies grow
In Flanders fields.

His poem was read far and wide. When the war finally ended, on November 11, 1918, people everywhere celebrated the return to peace.

A poppy is to remember
those far from home,
crossing troubled lands

and threatening waters

and dangerous skies.

It is for the wounded,
and those who cared for them.

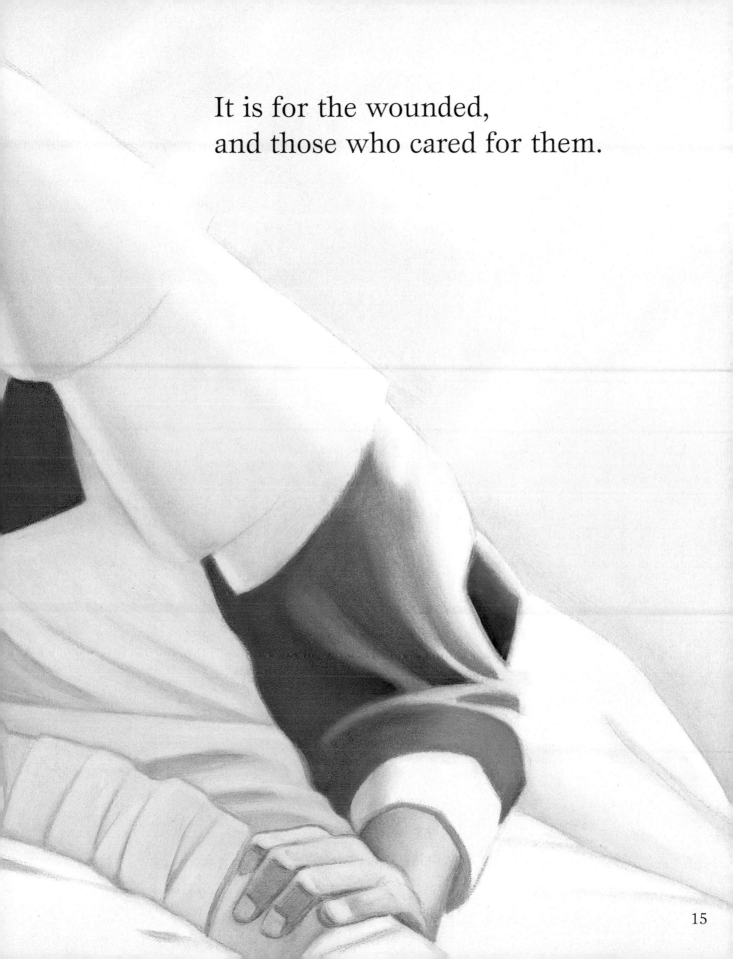

It is for the dead, and those
who carried on without them.

17

It is for the brave ones who remain,
and their memories of battle.

A poppy is for peace.

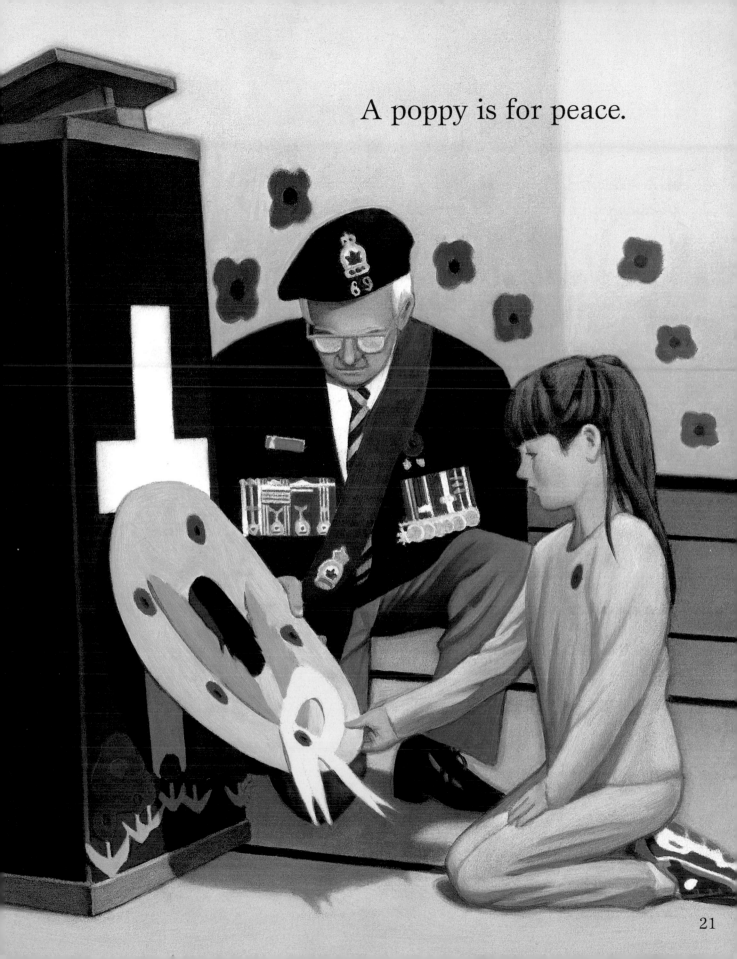

Every year on
Remembrance Day
it blooms across our land.

A poppy is to remember.

The Story of the Poppy

The wild red poppy of Flanders sprang up on the muddy battlefields and around the graves of those who fought in the First World War. This dreadful four-year struggle began in 1914 and ended in 1918. Over 600,000 Canadians and almost 12,000 Newfoundlanders crossed the ocean to serve in what was called "the war to end all wars."

Dr. John McCrae from Guelph, Ontario, was among those at the Second Battle of Ypres, in the region of Belgium known as Flanders. The conflict lasted four long weeks. John McCrae, a medical officer, treated an endless stream of wounded at his dressing station. In the early morning of May 2, 1915, his friend, Lieutenant Alexis Helmer, was killed.

Somehow on that bleak day, after his friend had been buried and the grave marked by a wooden cross, John McCrae took the time to reflect. Somehow in the midst of war, he found strength and beauty and hope, and wove them into a poem called "In Flanders Fields."

Seven months later the poem was published in England, and people took its ringing words into their hearts. In 1917 lines from the poem were used on Canadian posters to raise money for the war effort.

John McCrae did not live to see the world return to peace. He died of meningitis and pneumonia on January 28, 1918. Nine and a half months later, the Great War came to an end on Armistice Day, November 11, 1918.

During a pause in helping the wounded, Lieutenant-Colonel John McCrae wrote "In Flanders Fields" following the death of a close friend.

Just two days before the war ended, an American woman named Moina Belle Michael happened to read "In Flanders Fields." She decided that the poppy should be worn over the heart as a symbol of tribute and support for war veterans. For the rest of her life she worked to make this happen, arranging for disabled veterans to make the poppies. The profits from their sale would go to help veterans or their dependants.

In 1920 another enterprising woman, Anna E. Guérin of France, met Moina Belle Michael. She began to organize the production of handmade poppies in France, to be sold every year around the time of the armistice. The money raised would help poor children in areas of Europe that had been damaged by the war.

The next year Madame Guérin visited Canada, and her idea took root, as it had in other countries. Canada's Great War Veterans' Association officially adopted the poppy as its symbol of remembrance in November of 1921.

For many years, in the weeks leading up to Remembrance Day, The Royal Canadian Legion has distributed poppies all across our nation. The money raised helps veterans and their families, and goes to other worthy causes. Worn proudly over the heart, each poppy honours the courage and commitment of the hundreds of thousands of Canadians who have made great sacrifices to preserve our way of life.

Caitlin Manktelow places her poppy on a Calgary cenotaph after the moment of silence on Remembrance Day.

Canadian veterans walk Juno Beach at the ceremony marking the 60th anniversary of D-Day, June 6, 2004.

Remembrance Day in Canada

Canada's first Remembrance Day service was held at 11 o'clock on November 11, 1919. It began as a way to honour those people who had given their lives in the Great War — more than 65,000 of them. A minute of silence across the land marked the end of the war exactly one year before, at the 11th hour of the 11th day of the 11th month. Originally called Armistice Day, the name was officially changed to Remembrance Day in 1931.

Though people believed that war on such a huge scale could never happen again, the Second World War broke out in Europe in 1939 and lasted until 1945. Remembrance Days in Canada added to their honour roll the more than one million Canadians who served in World War II. Some came home safely, but many died at Dieppe and other battlegrounds far from home. Others were lost in the skies and at sea.

We also honour the courageous nurses who comforted and healed the wounded, and the farm, factory and office workers who did their part for the war effort. We remember the families who scrimped on food and skimped on fuel, and went without luxuries so that soldiers would be better clothed and fed.

We think of the wives and mothers who hid their worry, packing welcome parcels for loved ones overseas: hand-knitted socks, chocolate bars and cheerful letters. We honour those who opened their doors to

Hundreds of people stand silently before the immense Vimy Memorial as it is unveiled on July 26, 1936. Thousands of Canadian soldiers lost their lives at Vimy. The French nation gave Canada the land for the memorial, out of gratitude for Canada's help during World War I.

Private Jack Bernard, of the Duke of Connaught's Own Rifles, says goodbye to
his five-year-old son Warren as he marches off to war, New Westminster, B.C., 1940.

the awful news that their brother, son or
husband was missing in action or had
been killed.

But the Second World War was not
the last. From 1950 to 1953 Canadian
troops fought in the Korean War, far
away on the other side of the world.
We remember their gallant efforts on
Remembrance Day as well.

In 1956 Lester B. Pearson proposed
to the United Nations that troops be sent
to the Middle East to avert a war there.
For this, Pearson, who later became
Canada's prime minister, was awarded
the Nobel Peace Prize. Over the years,
Canadian forces have earned a reputation
as peacekeepers in many regions of
unrest around the world, a tradition
they proudly maintain today.

Thousands of postcards such as these kept families in
touch with their loved ones overseas during World War I.

The Truro Royal Canadian Legion Colour Party marches past during Remembrance Day ceremonies in Truro, Nova Scotia, in 2002.

As we approach Remembrance Day every year, we are reminded of all these efforts. We buy poppies to pin on our coats — to aid the veterans who have returned home. We go to school assemblies, where poems are read, poppies worn, and wreaths displayed. A veteran might put on his uniform and visit a school to tell his story — lest we forget. On November 11, at 11 o'clock, Canadians young and old, from sea to sea, observe two minutes of silence.

A remembrance service is held at the National War Memorial in Ottawa. Veterans across the country march in proud and solemn lines to town halls, cenotaphs and cemeteries, where poppy wreaths are laid for the fallen. At 11 o'clock, the moment of silence begins, and often a quiet tear is shed as we reflect on the sacrifices made.

Together on Remembrance Day we take the time to think of those Canadians

A girl places flowers among dozens of wreaths during Remembrance Day ceremonies in Sooke, British Columbia, in 2002.

who have given so much. We pledge to remember what they fought for — freedom and a world at peace. We think of the Canadians today who strive to foster peace in troubled regions of the world. In one special silent moment, we pledge to do the same.